W9-BSN-522

MISSION: MARS

PASCAL LEE

SCHOLASTIC INC.

For Laurence and Oliver
May they explore

Acknowledgments:
I would like to thank my editor, Mona Chiang, for the opportunity to write this book. Without her inspiration, vision, and patience, it would not exist. I am also grateful to many colleagues, friends, and members of my family for their support, in particular Buzz Aldrin, Joe Amarualik, Shannon Atkinson, Ben Audlaluk, Marc Boucher, Steve Braham, Mike Crowder, Edna DeVore, Terry Fong, Brian Glass, Ryan Hobson, Ed Hodgson, Steve Hoffman, Christopher Hoftun, Belgacem Jaroux, Brage Johansen, Tom Jones, Debbie Kolyer, Aalon Lee, Basil Lee, Claudia Lee, Marco Lee, Monique Lee, Vanessa Lee, Kira Lorber, Gary Martin, Chris McKay, Randy Miller, Armando Morales, Elon Musk, Tom Pierson, John Schutt, Mike Sims, Elaine Walker, Jesse Weaver, Mark Webb, Paul Wheelock, Alex Whitworth, Michael Wing, Pete Worden, Kris Zacny, Cookie, Ping Pong, and Skibo.

Editor: Mona Chiang
Designer: Ryan Hobson
Additional design support: Janet Kusmierski, Dave Neuhaus
Production editor: Annie McDonnell
Copy editor: Veronica Ambrose
Proofreader: Jody Revenson
Contracts manager: Karen Zubin
Visual resources: Steven Diamond, Dwayne Howard, Jeff Paul
Manufacturing: Joanna Croteau, Katheryn K. Gao, Jacob Kessler
Special assistant: Yoda

Illustrations: Cover and original works by Ryan Hobson based on design concepts by Pascal Lee. Illustrations © Pascal Lee except: p. 4: solar system © Scholastic; p. 13: chart © Scholastic; p. 43: Mars © Scholastic. Map on p. 11 by Jim McMahon © Scholastic.

Photos: Courtesy of Pascal Lee: cover: background, painting; p. 1: rovers; pp. 3, 5, 11, 17, 45, 47: author/Marco Lee; p. 9: author, rock; p. 27: spacesuit test: NASA/Pablo de Leon, HUD background; p. 31: K-10: NASA/Pascal Lee; p. 33: SEV: NASA/Pascal Lee; p. 35: author; p. 37: rock climbing: NASA/Kelly Snook; p. 39: Devon Island; p. 43: NASA/Brian Glass. Courtesy of Mars Institute: cover: author's photo; p. 10: desert, base, greenhouse; p. 11: astronauts; p. 25: author; p. 33: yellow rover. From NASA: pp. 2, 6, 21, 34: Mars; pp. 8 and 43: *Curiosity*; pp. 12, 21, 24, 26, 28, 30, 32, 36, 48: surface; p. 13: SLS; pp. 20, 22: Deimos; p. 21: Phobos; p. 36: Hellas Basin, Valles Marineris; p. 37: Olympus Mons; p. 38: sand sea, ice cap; p. 39: stealth region, valley networks; p. 40: lost city, bushes; p. 41: faces, elephant, Mars Bigfoot. Other sources: Cover: Mars rocks/Shutterstock Inc.; p. 2: background/Shutterstock Inc.; p. 6: Earth/Dreamstime; p. 7: warning sign/Dreamstime; p. 8: background/Dreamstime, map/Science Photo Library; p. 20: Asaph Hall/Corbis; p. 31: ATV: Mars Institute/Kawasaki Motors Corp., U.S.A.; p. 37: spacesuit: Spine Films/Josh Cassidy; p. 41: Earth's Bigfoot/Corbis.

No part of this publication may be reproduced, stored in a retrieval system, or transmitted in any form or by any means, electronic, mechanical, photocopying, recording, or otherwise, without written permission of the publisher. For information regarding permission, write to Scholastic Inc., Attention: Permissions Department, 557 Broadway, New York, NY 10012.

ISBN 978-0-545-56532-5

Copyright © 2013 Pascal Lee
All rights reserved. Published by Scholastic Inc.
SCHOLASTIC and associated logos are trademarks and/or registered trademarks of Scholastic Inc.

2 11 10 9 8 7 6 5 4 3 2 1   13 14 15 16 17 18/0

Printed in Mexico   49

First printing, September 2013

About page 1:
Field-testing in the Arctic.

Boldfaced vocabulary words in this book are defined in the glossary on page 48.

ATTENTION, NEW RECRUITS

Get ready for the greatest space mission of the century! The United States plans to send the first humans to Mars around 2035. That's years away, but preparations are already under way. It's not too early to join the adventure. Your mission: Begin Basic Training to become a Future Mars Explorer. Ready to start? Let's go!

YOUR TRAINING MISSION IS DIVIDED INTO SIX PHASES.

At the end of each phase, there's a training drill that tests your readiness for Mars. If you ace it, check the box and advance to the next phase. If you successfully complete the entire training mission, you'll be rewarded. Good luck!

MEET YOUR TRAINING DIRECTOR

Hi! I am Pascal Lee. I'm a planetary scientist and the chairman of the Mars Institute. For years, my colleagues and I have been researching ways to send humans to Mars. I will now help you prepare for this incredible journey. We'll be covering exploration methods, cool technology, and so much more! Throughout your training mission, look out for my Field Notes. In them, I'll let you in on some of my team's latest research and discoveries!

FUTURE MARS EXPLORER: GET READY FOR MARS!

DISCOVER MARS

WHERE'S MARS IN SPACE?

Mars is the fourth planet from the Sun and Earth's neighbor in space. Sometimes people call it the Red Planet because of the red color of its surface. No one knows who discovered Mars. But to the ancient Romans, the planet's color reminded them of blood and war. So they named it after Mars, their god of war.

Like all the other planets in the solar system, Mars orbits the Sun. The time it takes for a planet to complete one orbit is called a year. For Earth, that's 365.25 days. Mars travels at a slower pace than Earth. It also follows a wider loop around the Sun. So it takes Mars 687 Earth days (almost two Earth years!) to complete one orbit.

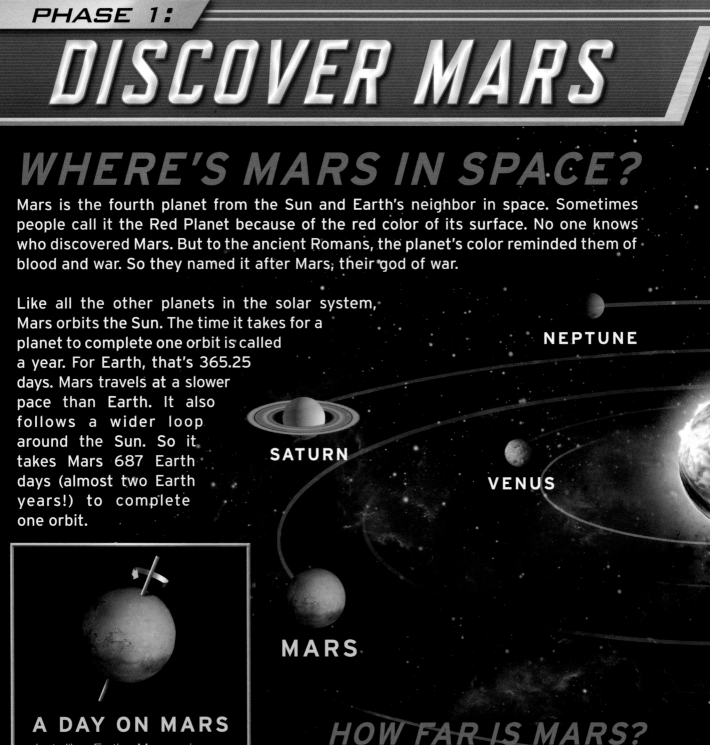

NEPTUNE

SATURN

VENUS

MARS

A DAY ON MARS

Just like Earth, Mars spins on its axis. One complete turn is a Martian day, or one sol. A sol lasts 24 hours and 37 minutes. That's almost exactly like a day on Earth: 24 hours. Lucky you! Because of this coincidence, your bedtime won't change by much!

HOW FAR IS MARS?

The distance between Earth and Mars changes all the time. When Earth passes between the Sun and Mars, the distance between the two planets is at its shortest. It can then be as short as 35 million miles (56 million kilometers). When Earth and Mars are on opposite sides of the Sun, they are at their farthest apart: about 250 million mi (400 million km). You can already tell that going to Mars will be a long trip!

MESSAGE FROM YOUR TRAINING DIRECTOR

Imagine setting foot on Mars. How mind-blowing that would be! Before we discuss how to get you to Mars, you'll need to learn some basics about the planet. Where is it? What dangers might you face there? Why would people want to go visit in the first place?

FUTURE MARS EXPLORER: BASIC TRAINING BEGINS!

WHY PICK MARS?

Jupiter, Saturn, Uranus, and Neptune are gas giants. They don't have a hard surface you can land on. They do have intriguing moons with solid surfaces, but all these worlds are too far to travel to for now.

Venus and Mercury are not far from Earth. They are terrestrial planets, meaning that, like Earth, they are rocky worlds with a hard surface. But they are too scorching hot to have any life on them, and too toasty for humans to explore.

This leaves Mars. It's close by. It has a solid surface, conditions that are almost similar to Earth, and chances of harboring life. This is why it's the first planet we should visit.

URANUS

JUPITER

MERCURY

MOON

N

EARTH

HOW FAR IS FAR?

EARTH   MOON

This picture shows the Earth-Moon system to scale. The Moon is about 250,000 mi (400,000 km) from Earth. When Mars is on the opposite side of the Sun from Earth, Mars is over 1,000 times farther away than our Moon!

If you could drive in space at 70 mi (113 km) per hour nonstop—not even to go to the bathroom—it would take you about five months to get to the Moon and about 5,000 months to get to Mars. That's close to 410 years! Advice: You'll need a spaceship that travels a lot faster than a car!

Solar system not to scale

DESTINATION MARS!

FIVE WAYS MARS ISN'T EARTH

1 LOW GRAVITY

Gravity is the main force that gives you your weight and keeps your feet on the ground. Gravity on Mars is only 38 percent of what it is on Earth. This weaker pull means that if you weigh, say, 100 pounds (45 kilograms) on Earth, you will feel like you weigh only 38 lbs (17 kg) on Mars. The weaker gravity also means that, with the same effort, you'll be able to leap 2.6 times higher on Mars than on Earth!

2 ALL LAND

Mars is about half the size of Earth. It has no oceans or seas. The planet is all land. The amount of land on Mars is about the same as all the land area on Earth combined!

3 MONSTER LANDFORMS

This planet has giant volcanoes, huge canyons, ancient dried-up rivers, and vast dune fields. Some are more than 10 times bigger than those on Earth! Mars also has a gazillion **impact craters**—all formed by countless **asteroids** and **comets** that have smashed into the planet since it was born 4.5 billion years ago.

4 INVISIBLE WATER

There is plenty of water on Mars, but most of it is out of sight. Where is it hiding? There's frozen water at the poles and buried in the ground. There's also water **vapor** in the air. But what about liquid water you could drink? Mars used to have lots of it near its surface, especially early in the planet's history. But it seems to have done a vanishing act. Maybe it's hiding deep underground.

5 GLOBAL DUST STORMS

Mars has a huge amount of dust, and this dust can get whipped into humongous dust storms. Dust storms start small, but some can grow and grow until they cover the entire planet. These global dust storms can last for weeks!

Let's take a closer look at the Red Planet. At first glance, Mars looks like a welcoming world. It has rocks and sand dunes, just like many national parks on Earth. But make no mistake. Mars is deadly. Thankfully, you'll have special gear to help you survive there. We'll talk about that later. For now, let's see what the planet is really like.

FIVE WAYS MARS IS DEADLY

SUFFOCATING AIR 1

Like Earth, Mars has an atmosphere. That's the layer of gas that surrounds the whole planet. Mars's atmosphere is made mostly of carbon dioxide. That's the gas that you exhale. If you try to breathe carbon dioxide, you would suffocate. The gas that you want to inhale is oxygen. Unfortunately, there's almost none in the Martian atmosphere.

SUPER LOW PRESSURES 2

Air is constantly pressing against your body and everything around you. You don't actually feel this **air pressure** on Earth because gases inside your body push out to make things feel balanced. Mars, unlike Earth, has very thin air. Its air pressure is super low. If you were exposed to it, the gases in your body would not be balanced. Instead, they would push out and expand. Your body would bubble up like a shaken can of soda!

FREEZING TEMPERATURES 3

Mars is crazy cold. Although temperatures can reach about 70 degrees Fahrenheit (20° Celsius) in the summer at the equator, they are normally around -80°F (about -60°C). In winter at the poles, it's -225°F (about -140°C)! You would turn into a human popsicle!

CHOKING HAZARDS 4

This planet looks red because it's covered in red dust. The dust is red because it contains rust. Mars is a very dusty, rusty place! Martian dust is very fine-grained and the rust is super corrosive. If you breathe it in, it will clog up your lungs and burn away at their tissue. You'd choke to death!

ZAPPING RAYS 5

Mars is constantly zapped by high-energy radiation from the Sun and from deep space. Mars's atmosphere helps block some of it, but not all. This radiation will penetrate your body and damage your cells. Over time, it could cause cancer, and even death.

ALIENS ON MARS?

Mars is a strange and dangerous place for humans. But could other forms of life be hanging out there? Do Martians exist? A big job for future Mars explorers will be to help find out.

Just a century ago, people thought that Mars was home to an alien civilization. Astronomers used to observe Mars with poor telescopes. They thought they saw lots of crisscrossing straight lines on the planet. They figured that those lines were canals that intelligent aliens had built for irrigation. The Martians were thirsty!

As it turns out, the canals were optical illusions. In 1971, *Mariner 9* became the first robotic spacecraft to orbit Mars. It took pictures of the entire planet from space and found it to be a giant desert. It saw no sign of any alien civilization. No animals. No plants. No life.

So does this mean that Martians don't exist? Maybe there's more to life on Mars than meets the eye . . . .

EARLY MARS EXPLORERS

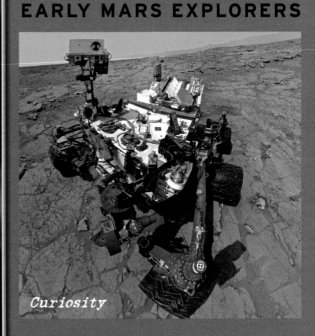

Curiosity

When you land on Mars, look out for robotic spacecraft that have arrived before you. The first one to ever touch Martian soil was *Mars 2*. It was launched by the former Soviet Union in 1971.

Unfortunately, it landed with a thud. Others followed. Many were very successful in exploring Mars. One of the most recent arrivals is the NASA *Curiosity* **rover**. It landed in 2012 to search for chemical signs of life.

GRAND CANALS

In the 1870s, Italian astronomer Giovanni Schiaparelli drew many maps showing the "waterways" on Mars. Here's an example.

MICROBE DETECTIVE

In spite of how harsh Mars is, there is still hope we might find life there. That's because we find life on Earth even in the harshest deserts. In these extreme environments, no big animals or large plants can survive. But some hardy **microbes** can. These bugs are called *extremophiles*. Might there be extremophiles hiding on Mars, too?

An important clue to finding life on Earth is liquid water. All Earth life needs liquid water, including microbes. If Martian microbes crave liquid water too, then your best bet to find them is to do what NASA calls "Follow the Water." You need to check out places on Mars where there is, or once was, liquid water.

A number of robotic spacecraft have landed on Mars to "Follow the Water." They've found plenty of signs of past liquid water, like dried-up riverbeds. But so far, no sign of life. As a Mars Explorer, you'll need to look harder and go where no robot has ever gone before!

What happens if you do find alien life on Mars? That would be BIG news! It would tell us that Earth is not the only planet with life in the universe. It would also tell us that life might be common out there.

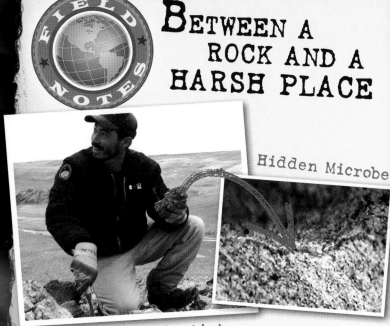

FIELD NOTES

BETWEEN A ROCK AND A HARSH PLACE

Hidden Microbe

Crouching Scientist

We go to the ends of the earth to learn how life can survive in extremely cold environments. For instance, here we are in the Arctic, in a seemingly lifeless landscape. After breaking open a rock with a hammer, we found green microbes hiding inside! For these microbes, the nooks and crannies of rocks are like caves for our ancestors: They provide shelter from the Sun, the cold, the wind, and the dryness. Would we find signs of life on Mars if we cracked open some rocks?

Time for your first drill! Let's see how well you know Mars.

1 If a person weighs 180 lbs (82 kg) on Earth, how heavy would he or she feel on Mars? (Use this formula to find out: Weight on Earth x 0.38)

2 Why is the dust on Mars red?

3 What's the term for hardy microbes that can survive in extreme environments?

Answers on page 48.

PREPARE FOR LAUNCH

MARS ON EARTH

The best way to prepare for Mars is to build experience living and working under conditions that are similar to Mars. Where would you do that? No place on Earth is exactly like Mars, but some places come close. They are called Mars **analogs**.

Cold, dry, barren, rocky, sandy, remote, and isolated places make the best Mars analogs. The Dry Valleys of Antarctica and Chile's Atacama Desert are the driest deserts on Earth. Both are almost as dry as Mars! In the United States, you'll find some very good analog sites, too: the deserts of the Southwest, the sand fields of Alaska, and the giant volcanoes of Hawaii.

HMPRS

SEE TWO "ASTRONAUTS" IN THIS PICTURE?

They are at Dumont Dunes in the Mojave Desert in California. They are practicing how to explore sand dunes because there are lots of them on Mars.

Greenhouse

MESSAGE FROM YOUR TRAINING DIRECTOR

Good job on completing Phase 1. Now that you're acquainted with Mars, let's get you ready for your voyage. A mission to Mars is no picnic. It will be the mother of all camping trips! Before you board your rocket, you'll have a lot to plan and train for.

FUTURE MARS EXPLORER: TIME TO PRACTICE, PRACTICE, PRACTICE!

FIELD NOTES

DEVON ISLAND

ARCTIC OCEAN

Devon Island

GREENLAND

North Pole

Haughton Crater

Baffin Bay

PACIFIC OCEAN

CANADA — Area of map

U.S. — ATLANTIC OCEAN

ARCTIC CIRCLE

0   200 MI
0   300 KM

Come visit one of the analogs where we help humans prepare for Mars! Devon Island, in the Arctic part of Canada, is 1,000 mi (1,610 km) from the North Pole. It's the largest uninhabited island on Earth. It has canyons, ancient dried-up rivers, ice, and even a meteorite impact crater: Haughton Crater. It's Mars on Earth! We come here to learn why Devon is so Mars-like, and how to explore Mars in the future.

My research team has set up a base right next to the crater: the Haughton-Mars Project Research Station (HMPRS). Like a future Mars base, the HMPRS has a greenhouse. Why? Mars explorers will want to eat fresh veggies every now and then. And you can't just grow lettuce outdoors on Mars. Our experimental greenhouse works like a robot: It can grow food on its own!

Devon Island's rugged and icy terrain is great for testing future Mars gear: rovers, spacesuits, drills, and even shelters. We'll talk more about all this later in Phase 4.

Field Test

THE RIGHT STUFF

The most important thing to have with you on a trip to Mars is good crewmates. Why? You'll be millions of miles from home, cooped up in a tight spacecraft, and exposed to constant danger. Things could get rough.

NASA and other space agencies worldwide conduct experiments to figure out what makes a good crew member. They sometimes lock up small groups of volunteers in tight quarters for months. They then observe how well the volunteers get along and get things done—or don't.

Here are some qualities a Mars explorer should have. Start aiming to have the right stuff!

1 KNOWLEDGE
The Mars crew won't be very large, maybe seven people or so. That's not a lot to take on all these jobs: pilot, mechanic, navigator, cook, doctor, dentist, geologist, biologist, plumber, roboticist, spacesuit expert, systems engineer, plus backups for all these jobs! You'll need to learn many skills and wear lots of different hats (or helmets)!

2 HEALTH
The trip to Mars will be long and hard. The nearest hospital could be months away. You'll need to keep your body and mind in good shape.

3 MOTIVATION
It will take a lot of hard work to get to Mars. You'll need to really want to go, and keep aiming for it.

4 ADAPTABILITY
Things often don't go as planned. A spacecraft part might break or a crewmate might get hurt. You'll always need to remain cool and adapt to new plans.

5 ALTRUISM
This means unselfish behavior. Being far away from Earth, you will only have each other to depend on. You will need to be a good team player and always think of others before yourself.

MOST POWERFUL ROCKET EVER

OK. So you've trained in the most Mars-like places on Earth. And you have the right stuff to be a great Mars explorer. Time to look at how to send you to Mars!

To launch humans to the Red Planet, NASA is building the most powerful rocket ever! It's called the Space Launch System, or SLS. You need a big, powerful rocket because Mars is far away, and there's a lot of stuff to haul there.

How much stuff? Take food, for instance. Each person requires about 2.2 lbs (1 kg) of food per day. A crew of seven on a 2.5-year journey will need about 14,000 lbs (6,350 kg). That's the weight of an adult African elephant!

On top of food, there's other **cargo**. You'll need to bring water, fuel, a lot of equipment, and your spacecraft. In total, we're looking at about 1,800,000 lbs (816,500 kg). That's like 130 elephants!

As mighty as the SLS rocket will be, it won't be able to lift more than 286,000 lbs (130,000 kg) at a time. To get all your stuff to Mars, your mission will require seven SLS rocket launches! Holy woolly mammoth!

NASA SLS ROCKET
This version of the SLS will launch cargo. A smaller version will launch the crew. At liftoff, the larger SLS rocket will have the thrust, or pushing power, of over 34 Boeing 747 jumbo jets!

HOW HUMONGOUS IS THE NASA SLS?
Here's how the SLS stacks up next to other giants.

Space Shuttle
184.2 ft (56.14 m)
Rocket plane once used to launch astronauts to Earth orbit.

Boeing 747-8
250.2 ft (76.3 m)
World's longest passenger airliner.

Saturn V
363 ft (111 m)
Rocket once used to launch astronauts to the Moon.

SLS: Small version
321 ft (97.8 m)
Rocket that will launch the Mars crew.

SLS: Big version
384 ft (117 m)
Rocket that will launch Mars-bound cargo.

OFF TO MARS!

You don't just climb into a rocket and lift off to Mars. You will be taking part in a multiple-step operation. There are lots of different scenarios for going to Mars. These steps are based on what NASA is considering. Let's check out the sequence.

FUEL TANKS

1 ASSEMBLY REQUIRED

Four giant SLS rockets blast off to **low Earth orbit** (LEO), about 250 mi (400 km) above Earth. These rockets carry the parts of two Mars cargo ships. The ships get assembled robotically in LEO.

2 CARGO GOES FIRST

These unmanned cargo ships are packed with equipment and supplies that you'll need once you get to Mars. The ships depart for Mars about two years ahead of you. Make sure they've arrived OK before you head off to Mars!

3 MORE ASSEMBLY REQUIRED

About six months before your departure, two more giant SLS rockets blast off to LEO. They deliver the parts of your Mars crew ship, which then gets assembled robotically.

4 YOUR TURN TO LAUNCH

Your crew launches aboard a smaller version of the SLS rocket. You dock with the Mars crew ship and move onboard. You spend a few weeks checking out your Mars ship and settling in.

5 WE HAVE TMI!

Once you are ready to depart, press the Trans-Mars Injection (TMI) button. That will fire up your rocket engines and send you on your way to Mars. *Bon voyage!*

EARTH

FLORIDA

SOLAR PANELS

MARS LANDER
This is the space vehicle that you'll use to land on Mars.

EARTH RETURN VEHICLE
This "ERV" capsule will be attached to the Mars ship until the very last moment of your journey. You'll use it to reenter Earth's atmosphere and come home!

INFLATABLE HABITAT
This "i-Hab" is where you will spend most of your during your trip to Mars and back. Since it's inflat it can pack tightly for launch on an SLS rocket. in LEO, it expands into a roomy living space.

SERVICE MODULE
This section houses your Mars ship's support systems. That's the equipm and supplies (oxygen and water) neede keep your crew alive while onboard.

Let's see if you've mastered your ground training. Are the following statements true or false?

1 A Mars analog is located on Mars.

2 The SLS cargo rocket is larger than the *Saturn V* rocket.

3 You will arrive at Mars at the same time as the Mars cargo ships.

TRAINING DRILL

Answers on page 48.

NAVIGATE SPACE

FROM EARTH TO MARS

Your "road" to Mars is not so straightforward. Since Earth and Mars are constantly moving around the Sun, the most efficient way to travel is to loop around the Sun as well. Just follow a gentle arc connecting Earth's orbit to Mars's orbit. Using current technology, the trip could last as little as 6 months.

But, you better time your departure correctly! You need to calculate so that Mars will be in exactly the right place by the time you reach its orbit 6 months later. If you leave Earth too early or too late, Mars won't be there!

Once you get to Mars, you'll need to wait about 18 months (1.5 years) for Earth and Mars to get into position again. Then it's another 6 months to fly home. All in all, you'll be gone 30 months. That's 2.5 years! Better take some good reading with you!

18 MONT

RETURN TO EARTH

SUN

START HERE!

DEPART EARTH

After all that ground training, you'll be off to Mars! What a thrill! But you'll need to be prepared for a long and perilous journey ahead. In this phase, you'll discover what life might be like onboard your Mars ship. You'll also find out what dangers lurk in deep space. And what little "surprises" await you as you close in on Mars . . . .

FUTURE MARS EXPLORER: PREPARE FOR A WILD RIDE!

LONG-DISTANCE CALLS

Even though you're off to Mars, don't be a stranger! NASA's Mission Support, and pretty much everyone on planet Earth, will want to keep track of what you're doing. To communicate with Earth, you'll be using radio signals. That's both good news and bad news.

The good news is that radio signals travel at the **speed of light** (186,000 mi per second, or about 300,000 km per second). That's the fastest possible speed in nature. This means that when a friend says, "Wassup?" to you from Earth, you'll hear the greeting with as little time delay as possible.

The bad **news** is that "as little time delay as possible" could still mean a long delay. At the beginning of your trip, when you are still close to Earth, there will be almost no time delay. You can chat with your friend like you would on a phone. But as you get farther and farther away, the time delay will steadily increase.

By the time you get to Mars, your greetings will take a long time to reach the other person. Each way can take anywhere from 3 minutes (when Earth and Mars are at their closest to each other) to 22 minutes (when Earth and Mars are on opposite sides of the Sun). Instead of chatting with your friend, it will be like swapping voice mails!

S ON MARS

6 MONTHS

ARRIVE AT MARS

6 MONTHS

DEPART MARS

LIFE ABOARD YOUR MARS SHIP

How might you live as you travel to Mars? Life aboard won't be dull. For starters, you won't be standing still, but floating in **microgravity** (see right). You'll also have plenty to do, like planning your excursions on Mars, staying in good health, fixing things, and more. Let's take a tour of your Mars ship.

CHECK OUT THE FLIGHT DECK

While in transit between Earth and Mars, the ERV's cockpit will serve as the whole ship's control center. This will be the "brain" of your Mars ship!

SLURP YOUR FOOD

Float into the kitchen for a meal. Your "astronaut food" will come in microwavable pouches with a shelf life of 10 years! Warm it up, extend straw, squeeze, and slurp! Drink lots of water. By the way, it will be mostly recycled from crew sweat and urine!

SERVICE MODULE

EARTH RETURN VEHICLE

OPERATE THE WATERLESS LAUNDROMAT

Treat yourself to a load of laundry. How does it work? This model blasts dirty laundry with frozen carbon dioxide, or dry ice, pellets. The pellets then vaporize and scrub off dirt.

⚠ DANGER!

DODGE RADIATION

PROBLEM: You'll be zapped by dangerous radiation from the Sun and deep space.

SOLUTION: During bouts of extra-heavy radiation, hide inside the radiation shelter. It has protective lead walls. For everyday protection, line the i-Hab's walls with food and water. These items contain hydrogen, which dampens radiation. But as food gets consumed, hydrogen will end up in poop. To remain protected, save your poop in bags and use them to line your i-Hab's walls!

MICROGRAVITY

During most of your flight to Mars and back, you will be weightless because you'll be in free fall. Compared to gravity on Earth, which is 1 G, being weightless is being in zero G, or microgravity. How does this work?

Think of a human cannonball free-falling back to Earth after being shot out of a cannon.

Like this person, your Mars ship will be free-falling around the Sun after being "shot" away from Earth.

Anything loose inside the Mars ship, including you, will just float around.

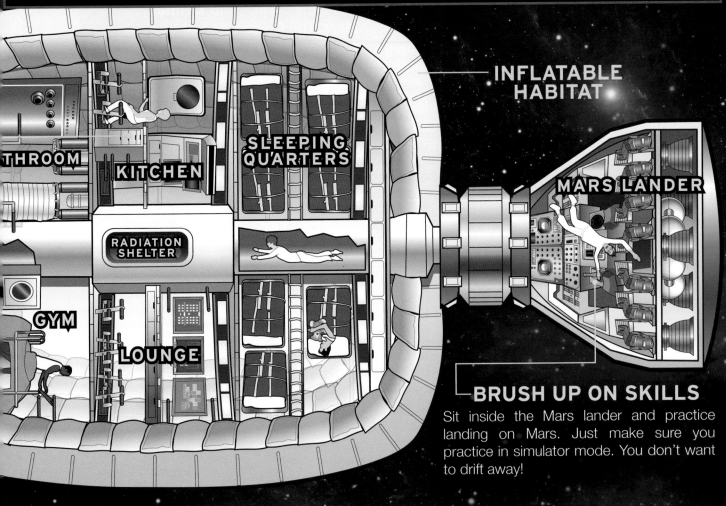

INFLATABLE HABITAT

BATHROOM

KITCHEN

SLEEPING QUARTERS

RADIATION SHELTER

GYM

LOUNGE

MARS LANDER

BRUSH UP ON SKILLS

Sit inside the Mars lander and practice landing on Mars. Just make sure you practice in simulator mode. You don't want to drift away!

FIGHT MICROGRAVITY

PROBLEM: Being in microgravity for months at a time is not good for your body. Three problems arise:

1. Your bones will lose calcium, the mineral that makes them strong. They'll become brittle.
2. Your muscles will get lazy and shrink.
3. Extra blood will flow to your head. The extra fluid pressure to your eyes will damage them.

SOLUTION: Exercising daily on a treadmill (with straps so you won't float away!) will help with 1 and 2. Space doctors are still wondering how to prevent 3.

ISLANDS OFF MARS!

Finally, you'll close in on Mars. But surprise! It's not alone. It's accompanied by what looks like two giant potatoes! No need to worry! They are Phobos and Deimos, the two moons of Mars.

These moons are small. Phobos is only 17 mi (27 km) long, and Deimos merely 9 mi (15 km). The only thing worrisome about them is their names. If you speak Greek, you'll know that **Phobos** means "fear," and **Deimos** means "terror." Why such ominous names? Mars, the Roman god of war, was known as Ares in Greek mythology. This Ares character had two combat-happy sons: Phobos and Deimos.

The two moons of Mars are very close to the planet. How close? Deimos orbits at a distance of 14,580 mi (23,460 km) from Mars. Phobos is even closer. It is just 5,827 mi (9,377 km) away. That's like 42 times closer than our Moon is from Earth!

A HALL OF FAME

No one knows who discovered Mars. But we know who discovered its moons: Asaph Hall.

American astronomer Asaph Hall (1829–1907) was born in Goshen, Connecticut. He was just 13 years old when his father died. To help support his family, he left school at age 16 and began working as a carpenter. But Hall was eager to continue learning, so he studied on his own. He eventually became a math teacher.

Hall was very interested in astronomy, a subject that can require a lot of math. In 1862, President Abraham Lincoln appointed Hall professor of mathematics at the U.S. Naval Observatory in Washington, D.C. At the time, the observatory had one of the biggest telescopes in the world. In August 1877, while looking through it, Hall discovered two little moving dots right next to Mars: Phobos and Deimos!

Asaph Hall

DEIMOS

PHOBOS PHOBIA

Phobos is so close to Mars that it's slowly drifting toward the planet. One day, Phobos will fall out of the sky! But there's more.

As Mars's gravity pulls Phobos in, it's also yanking the moon apart! That's maybe why Phobos has grooves: They might be cracks from it breaking up. Phobos will eventually crumble into a trail of debris spread along its orbit around Mars. The planet will then have a ring, just like Saturn. Over time, each piece of Phobos will fall on Mars. Yikes!

Future Mars Explorer: Have no fear! You don't have to watch your head. The debris from Phobos won't rain down on Mars for another 10 to 50 million years!

PHOBOS

PIT STOP AT PHOBOS

Phobos and Deimos are mysterious small worlds. They will be amazing places for you to explore! Let's start with Phobos.

Imagine putting on a spacesuit and jet-packing to its surface. From this inner moon, you'll have an incredible view of the Red Planet. Phobos is so close to Mars that the planet will appear about 6,400 times larger than our own Moon as seen from Earth! Check out some of the exciting things you can do on Phobos.

DUSTY DEIMOS

This outer moon is just as interesting to explore. But be careful! Deimos could be covered in a lot of dust, so you might not be able to anchor yourself securely.

PHOBOS ROCKS

Go rock hunting. The rocks on Phobos could be among the oldest in the solar system, maybe up to 4.5 billion years old! Look out for chunks of Mars, too. Why? When big asteroids and comets hit Mars, bits and pieces of the planet can get tossed into space. Some might have landed on Phobos. If you're lucky, you might find traces of ancient life inside Mars rocks, now sitting on Phobos.

HOOKED ON PHOBOS

To work on the surface without bouncing around, you need to get a grip. How? Anchor yourself to Phobos. Just place your anchor driver against the ground and screw an anchor into position. When you're ready to move on, unscrew the anchor, and off you go.

PARK AND GO!

Your Mars ship is orbiting Mars at about 3,716 mi (5,980 km) above its surface. It is flying in formation with Phobos, "parked" only 1.5 mi (about 2.5 km) off of the small moon.

GIANT LEAPS FOR MANKIND

Phobos is so small that its gravity is 1,700 times weaker than on Earth. You must realize the gravity of this situation! If you try to walk, you'll make big bounces. If you push hard on your legs, you could jump a mile high. If you're not careful, you might even drift away!

SEARCH AND RECOVERY

Perhaps you'll be sent to find an old robotic spacecraft. It may have collected rock and soil samples from Mars long before your own mission. It then parked itself on Phobos, waiting for you to retrieve the precious samples. Opening this "treasure chest" will be exciting and fun!

TRAINING DRILL

How well did you navigate through this phase? See if you can answer the following questions.

1 How fast do radio signals travel?

2 Where in your Mars ship should you hide at times of extra-heavy radiation?

3 What are Phobos and Deimos?

Answers on page 48.

GEAR UP FOR SURVIVAL

LANDING ON MARS

With the Mars ship parked in orbit, the entire crew will squeeze into the Lander and prepare for EDL. That means Entry, Descent, and Landing. The whole EDL sequence lasts just a few minutes, but it'll be one of the hairiest parts of your mission. One wrong move could mean *game over* for the whole crew. Ready for EDL? Buckle up!

Altitude
····· **250 MI**
(400 KM)

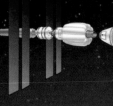

80 MI
(130 KM)

5 MI
(7.3 KM)

1 SEPARATE LANDER

Your Lander has been attached to the Mars ship since your departure from Earth. To separate from the Mars ship, fire up small thrusters. Then down to Mars you go!

2 ENTER ATMOSPHERE

You'll be entering Mars's atmosphere at a speed of 7,800 mi (12,500 km) per hour! As the Lander rubs against Martian air, it experiences friction and starts to slow down. This **atmospheric friction** also heats up the Lander and the air around it. You'll see a pink glow outside your windows. Quite a way to make an entry!

3 TAKE THE HEAT

The lower you go, the thicker the atmosphere gets. Friction soon becomes so intense that your Lander's underside reaches 4,000°F (2,200°C)! You'll be engulfed in a ball of fire! Thankfully, your Lander is equipped with a heat shield that keeps it, and you guys, cool!

4 OPEN PARACHUTES

Your Lander has slowed down enough, and the air is now thick enough, for parachutes to work. It's time to pop them open. These giant fabric structures trap air. This creates extra friction to further slow you down.

The big moment has arrived! It's now time to prepare you for your meeting with Mars. This part of your trip will be filled with even more exciting experiences. But you'll also face many dangers. To survive, you'll need to learn how to operate some important equipment. Check out some of the latest design concepts. You are getting an advance peek!

FUTURE MARS EXPLORER: TIME TO TEST OUT SOME GEAR!

2 MI (3.21 KM)

1 MI (1.6 KM)

5 DROP HEAT SHIELD

As you continue your descent, let go of the heat shield. It will just drop off and crash on Mars. Instruments tucked beneath the Lander, like ones that can measure your distance from the ground, will now kick into action. They will guide you to your final landing.

6 PARACHUTES AWAY

Your parachutes have done a good job: They've slowed you down a lot. But it's now time to get rid of them! For a moment, you'll drop like a rock. But no worries! Something beefier is about to step in to help you land.

7 ENGINES IGNITE

Your Lander's rocket engines come on. You'll now be able to maneuver your Lander. You'll have a couple of minutes to look around and pick out a safe landing site. Search for a spot that's flat and free of boulders and ditches.

8 TOUCHDOWN!

Found the perfect spot? Prepare for Landing! You'll know that you're very close to the ground when you see dust swirling outside your windows. Then, with a gentle thump, your ground contact lights will come on. Your rocket engines will shut down. **YOU WILL BE ON MARS!**

0.6 MI (1 KM)

0 MI (0 KM)

SUIT UP!

Time to gear up for your first spacewalk on Mars! A spacesuit is more than just clothing. Think of it as a wearable spacecraft. It protects your body from Mars's deadly environment. It's also packed with equipment, even computers, to help you explore. Time to try it on!

HELMET

A large visor will give you an awesome view of things. Use the sunshade and dust wiper to keep your visor clear. (Try not to sneeze. There are no wipers inside!) Need a snack? Use the built-in straws to slurp food or sip water.

CONTROLS

This box allows you to control conditions inside your suit, like air pressure and temperature. Adjust as necessary.

WHY IS THE SUIT DARK BLUE?

The dark color absorbs more sunlight to help you stay warm. The blue color makes you stick out in an orange landscape.

WRIST DISPLAY

This touch-screen device can display handy information, like a checklist or a repair manual.

BOOTS AND GAITERS

These sturdy boots can handle all sorts of Martian terrain—from soft sand to sharp rocks. Your initials will be carved into their treads. This way, your footprints can be identified! The "leg warmers" above your boots are actually gaiters. They are covers designed to protect your pants from getting shredded by sharp rocks!

VIEW FROM INSIDE

Your computer inside your spacesuit will use your visor as a screen. With this "Head-Up Display," you'll be able to look outside, and at the same time, keep an eye on your suit's oxygen level, view maps, get directions, and track everyone's position.

CAMERAS

Cameras will record what you see in 3-D. This way, people on Earth can follow all your exciting adventures!

BACKPACK

The backpack's technical name is Portable Life Support System, or PLSS for short. (Pronounced "pliss," please!) It contains all the spacesuit machinery to keep you alive: oxygen and water tanks, batteries, cooling fans, etc. Your PLSS opens up in the back like a refrigerator door. That's how you get into, and out of, your spacesuit.

WHAT'S UNDERNEATH?

Your spacesuit will be made of many fabric layers. Each one protects you from a different danger on Mars: low air pressure, extreme temperatures, **micrometeorites**, UV rays, dust, etc.

The Mars Suit Challenge

Designing a spacesuit for Mars is no easy engineering feat! Here I am testing a spacesuit in a simulated Martian dust storm. Basically, I was being pelted by dust. We discovered that even the smallest grains could damage spacesuit fabric. So we need to develop a material that is sturdy and can put up with Martian dust.

In addition, the spacesuit used for walking on the Moon won't do on Mars. Under the planet's gravity, that suit would feel like it weighs over 100 lbs (45 kg). Imagine lugging that around to climb rocks on Mars!

Spacesuit engineers are actively trying to find ways to lighten the load. My research team has come up with one idea. On page 30, you'll see how you don't have to carry all your oxygen supply. You'll get some help—on wheels!

HAB SWEET HAB

Where will you go on your first walk on Mars? Home! Very near your landing site will be another spacecraft. It's the Habitat, or "Hab." It was sent to Mars as cargo before you left Earth. This is where you'll be living.

Your Hab will have three decks. It will be filled with enough oxygen for you to breathe and live in shirtsleeves. Let's take a tour!

GARAGE AND TUNNEL

The garage will be an airlock just like the other exit. It will have a giant door with a ramp for small rides to drive off. It will also have a small door connected to an inflatable tunnel. Walk through here—like how you would board an airplane—to get into a bigger ride parked outside.

SLEEPING QUARTERS

SHOWER

FUEL TANKS

TUNNEL

EXIT HERE

To go for a walk, you can't just open the door and step out. You must first go through an airlock. It's an airtight chamber in which you can change the air pressure to match the low pressure outside on Mars or the higher pressure inside the Hab.

WATER TANKS

UPPER DECK

Here's where you'll find the control center, the "brain" of your mission. It's where you'll communicate with Earth and check on the conditions inside the Hab. It's also where you'll keep track of your crewmates while they explore outside. Your personal bedroom is up here, too!

CONTROL CENTER

MID DECK

This is where you'll hang out with your crewmates. The level has a kitchen, a dining area, and a lounge. During your time off, you can relax here and watch movies on a big screen. You'll also find a shower, a toilet, and a "hospital." There's also space to store food and other supplies (like toilet paper!).

HOSPITAL

LOUNGE

LOWER DECK

This is the work floor. It has a spacesuit maintenance room, a garage, labs to study rock samples, and a gym. Old fuel tanks used for the Hab's landing are now used to store oxygen and water.

SPACESUIT ROOM

AIRLOCK

Once you're in your spacesuit, lower the pressure in the airlock until it's the same as outside. Then walk out. When you return to the Hab, enter the airlock and repressurize it. Then get out of your spacesuit. If you forget to repressurize, it will be like removing your spacesuit outside: a deadly mess!

FOUR-WHEELING ON MARS!

Now we'll check out all your cool wheels on Mars! You'll have not one, but two types of rovers. The first type is the ATV, or All-Terrain Vehicle. This small, personal rover is an open vehicle. So you must wear a spacesuit to drive it.

You may have seen similar-looking ATVs on Earth. But your Mars ATV will be different: It'll be smart! It can be remote-controlled or even drive itself, like an intelligent robot. Let's go for a spin.

CONTROLS

To make your ATV go, press the green accelerator button. To slow down, just release the button. A display panel between the handlebars shows important information, like your ATV's speed and fuel levels.

STORAGE BOX

Store samples here. Put spare parts, tools, and other exploration gear in the rear storage box.

VIDEO CAMERAS

Your ATV has several video cameras. They allow everyone else to keep track of where the ATV is and where it's going. Here's one camera. Can you find the others?

ENGINE

Your ATV is powered by fuel cells. They work by combining hydrogen and oxygen, converting their chemical energy into electricity. The fuel cells, along with their oxygen and hydrogen tanks, are located here.

ANTENNA

This dish is used to communicate with Earth. It allows scientists there to remote control your ATV—just like how they drive the *Curiosity* rover on Mars.

TRANSFORMER SEATING

An ATV normally carries one person. But, in an emergency, transform it into a two-seater! Just remove this storage box and fold out a backseat. Your passenger will face backward and can share your ATV's oxygen supply.

OXYGEN SUPPLY

Remember how we need to make the Mars spacesuit lighter? When riding, just plug your backpack into an oxygen supply behind you. With this ability to charge up, you can walk around with just a small oxygen tank in your PLSS!

FAT TIRES

Wide tires and thick treads can handle both the rocky terrain and the soft sand on Mars.

Smart Car

How do we know that ATVs will be a good choice for Mars? My research team has been testing different ways to explore Devon Island. We found that the most efficient way to get around that Mars analog is to use ATVs.

The future Mars ATV will be smart in many different ways. You'll be able to send it out on its own to scout out dangerous paths. It will also follow you around as you explore Mars on foot. This way, its spare oxygen supply will always be handy in case you run short.

Scientists at NASA Ames Research Center are already engineering the brains of these future rovers. Here's NASA's brainy K-10, which did a test run on Devon Island. My K-9, Ping Pong, is impressed by what the K-10 can do!

THE MARS CAMPER

If you want to take off for several days, an ATV won't do. Your spacesuit and ATV can only carry a few hours' worth of oxygen. To make longer trips, you'll need the Pressurized Rover, or PR for short.

A PR is like a big motor home. It has an airtight cabin filled with oxygen to breathe. You'll drive, live, sleep, and work inside in shirtsleeves. Think of it as your Hab on wheels! Time to climb aboard!

GALLEY

Stock this small kitchen with food and water for your trip. What if the water tank runs dry? Start drinking recycled water—from the toilet!

COCKPIT

The pilot operates the PR from here. The navigator keeps track of your position and gives directions.

ROBOTIC ARMS

If you drive by a cool rock and don't have time for a spacewalk, pick it up with these robotic arms.

DOOR

TRAINING DRILL

How well do you know your gear? Let's find out.

1 At what altitude will your Lander enter Mars's atmosphere?

2 On which level of the Hab will you find your bedroom?

3 What's the power source for your exploration rovers?

Answers on page 48.

SPACESUIT PORTS

Need to go out for a spacewalk? Your spacesuit is already hanging outside, just behind this back wall. You enter your suit from inside the PR. Just open the suit port hatch, then your suit's backpack door. Slide into your spacesuit and close all doors behind you. You're now ready to walk off! When you come back, do everything in reverse. See here for an outside view of the spacesuit ports.

TOILET

To use the toilet, just draw a little curtain and go about your business. That's it for privacy and odor control!

OXYGEN TANKS

Make sure to carry enough oxygen to power the fuel cells and for breathing.

FUEL CELLS

Like your ATVs, your PR runs on fuel cells, only bigger ones!

Roving Around

How do you design the best possible PR for Mars? Lots of road tests! This is NASA's Space Exploration Vehicle (SEV).

I was lucky enough to field-test this experimental PR. The SEV is so nimble, it can make a complete turn over one spot. This ability will help you check out very tight spots on Mars.

To really experience what a PR trip on Mars will be like, my teammates and I go on long rover trips across extreme wilderness. We drove this yellow Humvee rover hundreds of miles on sea ice. The trip was hair-raising. At one point, the rover almost fell through the ice! It also got stuck in deep snow a few times—just like how you might get stuck in sand on Mars. Lesson learned: Plan carefully. A PR drive on Mars will be even more dangerous.

EXPLORE THE RED PLANET

MARS MAP

This map highlights major areas and great places to visit. Use the coordinates (letters at the bottom, numbers on the left) to locate things. For example, the coordinates for Hellas Basin are (C, 6). Can you find it where column C and row 6 intersect? Keep practicing using coordinates. You'll need to refer to this map throughout this phase.

MAP KEY

- Seven Wonders of Mars
- Weirdest Attractions
- Rovers that landed in the 21st century

EXPLORATION TIP!

You'll be spending a lot of time studying rocks and soil. Keep these tools handy!

- **Hammer**, to break apart rocks
- **Drill**, to extract samples from underground
- **Microscope camera**, to examine things up close
- **Containers**, to store samples

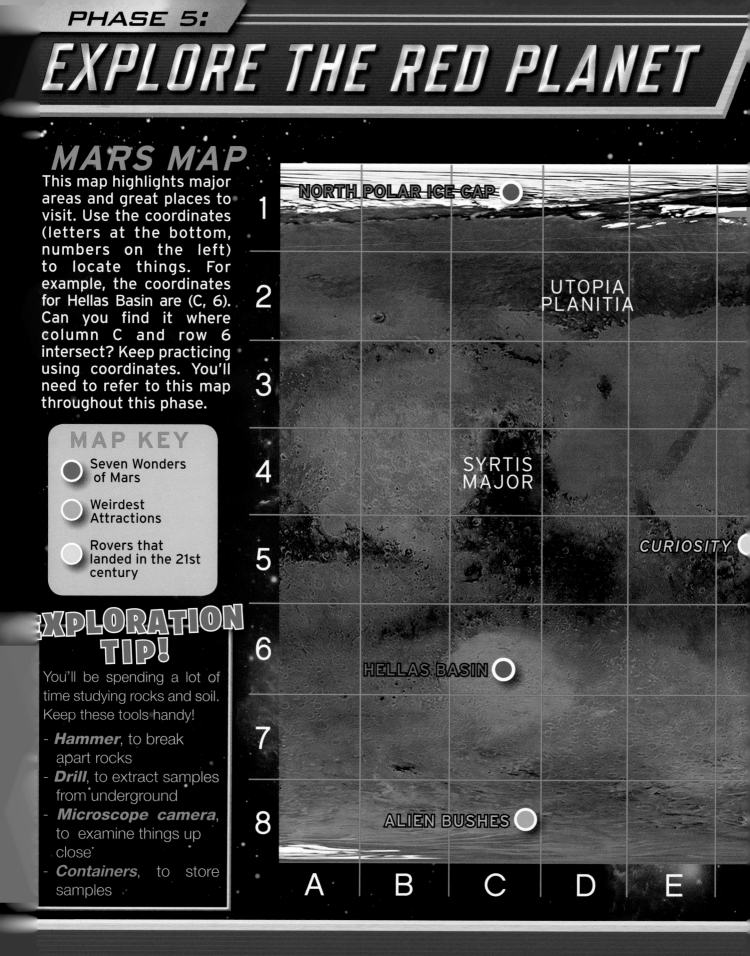

NORTH POLAR ICE CAP

UTOPIA PLANITIA

SYRTIS MAJOR

CURIOSITY

HELLAS BASIN

ALIEN BUSHES

1 2 3 4 5 6 7 8

A B C D E

MESSAGE FROM YOUR TRAINING DIRECTOR

Now that you know how to work your gear, let's prepare to explore Mars! Before you hop into your rover, you need to know how to find things on a map. In this phase, you'll locate and explore some of the most awesome spots on Mars. I'll also be giving you some exploration tips along the way.

FUTURE MARS EXPLORER: LET'S ROLL!

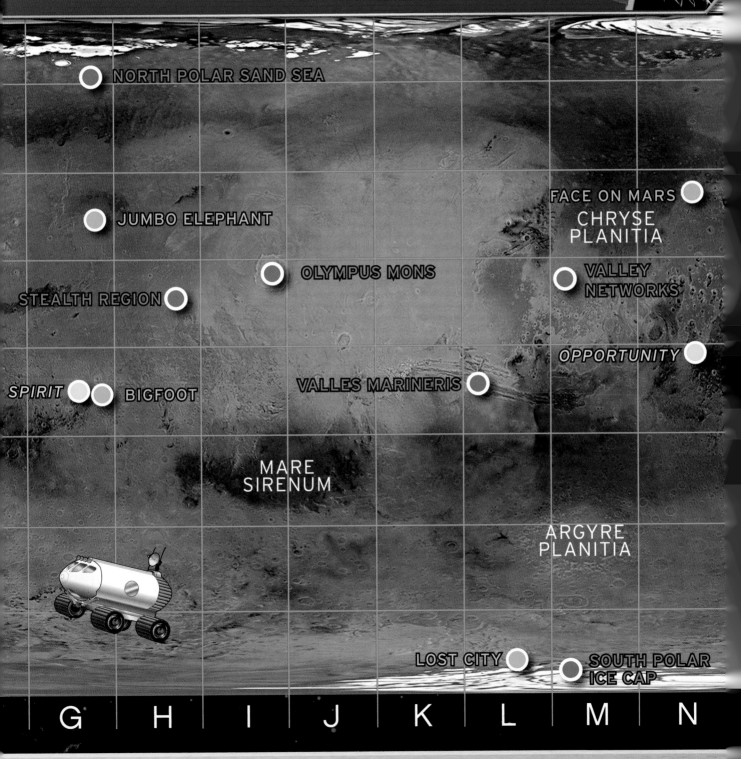

NORTH POLAR SAND SEA

JUMBO ELEPHANT

FACE ON MARS
CHRYSE
PLANITIA

OLYMPUS MONS

VALLEY
NETWORKS

STEALTH REGION

OPPORTUNITY

SPIRIT BIGFOOT

VALLES MARINERIS

MARE
SIRENUM

ARGYRE
PLANITIA

LOST CITY

SOUTH POLAR
ICE CAP

G   H   I   J   K   L   M   N

THE SEVEN WONDERS OF MARS

There will be a lot for you to explore on Mars. You won't have time to see everything, but try to visit these seven amazing places. Not only are they impressive in size and nature, they all connect to the story of water on Mars. As you learned earlier, you will need to "Follow the Water" to search for life!

HERE!

1 HELLAS BASIN
Claim to Fame: Biggest Crater
Map coordinates: C, 6

This gigantic hole in the ground measures 1,400 mi (2,250 km) wide and about 4.5 mi (7.2 km) deep. It formed about 4 billion years ago when a giant asteroid hit Mars. KABOOM!

Explore the edge of this crater and look for ancient hot springs. When the asteroid hit, the ground got superhot. Water in the ground came gushing out. These hot springs are now cold and dry. But back then, they would have been cozy spots for microbes. Be sure to look for signs of heat-loving extremophiles.

3 VALLES MARINERIS
Claim to Fame: Deepest and Longest Canyon
Map Coordinates: L, 5

This giant crack in the ground is 2,500 mi (4,000 km) long, 120 mi (200 km) wide, and 4 mi (6.5 km) deep. How big is that? Almost as wide as the United States mainland!

This dried-out canyon used to contain water and ice, but that was a while ago. The walls of the canyon have rock layers that are even more ancient. Check out these layers up close to sleuth for **fossil** microbes.

Warning: Watch your step! The slopes of Valles Marineris are very steep, and prone to landslides! The canyon can get foggy, too.

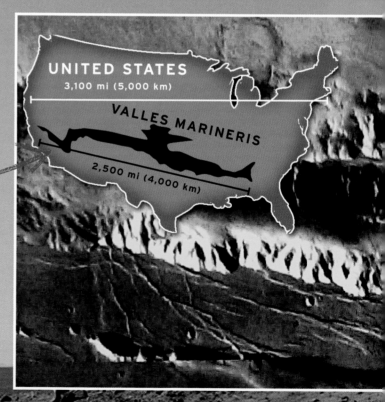

UNITED STATES
3,100 mi (5,000 km)

VALLES MARINERIS
2,500 mi (4,000 km)

OLYMPUS MONS

2

Claim to Fame:
Tallest Mountain
Map coordinates: I, 4

The tallest mountain on Mars is also the tallest in the entire solar system! This giant reaches a height of 14 mi (23 km). Earth's tallest mountain, Mount Everest, is puny in comparison. It's just 5.5 mi (8.8 km) high.

But that's not all. Olympus Mons is a volcano! It's of a type called shield volcano. That's because it's shaped like an old warrior's shield: round, slightly dome-shaped, and spread out. In fact, it's 370 mi (600 km) wide! Olympus Mons is not erupting right now, but it might still be active—just dormant.

There are caves on the sides of the volcano. See if they are damp and warm like some caves on Earth. Look around to see if you can find microbes hiding inside.

OLYMPUS MONS: 14 mi (23 km)   **MOUNT EVEREST: 5.5 mi (8.8 km)**

EXPLORATION TIP!

How do you examine rocks inside a steep canyon? Try rock climbing. Here, I help my brother Marco, our camp doctor, demonstrate scaling down a cliff on Devon Island. This is not an easy thing to do while wearing a spacesuit. You'll need to become an expert climber before attempting this on Mars.

Make sure you sift through the sand! We've collected samples from sand dunes on Earth that have traces of life. Might the dunes on Mars contain signs of life, too?

4 NORTH POLAR SAND SEA
Claim to Fame: Biggest Sandbox
Map Coordinates: G, 1

Drive north! Just before you reach the north polar ice cap of Mars, you'll find sand. Lots of it! The north polar ice cap is surrounded by a 2,000-mi (3,200-km)-long band of sand dunes. This sand covers an area the size of the state of Texas!

There's a hidden treasure buried beneath the sand: ice. Massive amounts of ice! The sand protects the ice and keeps it cold. Dig through the sand and see what you find. Any microbes, dead or alive, trapped in the ice?

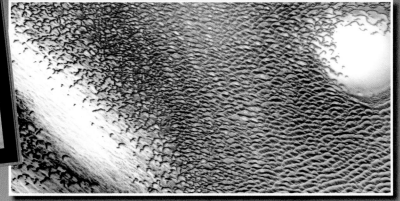

5 NORTH & SOUTH POLAR ICE CAPS
Claim to Fame: Coldest Spots
Map Coordinates C, 1 and M, 8

Brave the extreme cold! In winter, temperatures at the north and south polar ice caps drop to -225°F (-140°C). How cold is that? A lot colder than the chilliest temperature ever recorded on Earth. That was -128.6°F (-89.2°C) measured in Antarctica on July 21, 1983.

If you head to Mars's ice caps to search for life, watch out! In winter, the ice caps are completely covered with frozen carbon dioxide, or dry ice (just like the stuff in your Mars ship's laundry machine). On Earth, dry ice is sometimes used in ice-cream trucks to keep the treats frozen. Dry ice is so cold that if you touch it, it can injure your skin!

6. STEALTH REGION
Claim to Fame: Top Secret Region
Map Coordinates: H, 4

This 125-mi (200-km)-wide area is very mysterious. It's called the Stealth Region because, like a stealth airplane, it's invisible to radar!

Radar is an instrument used to detect objects from a distance. Here's how: The radar sends a signal to an object. Then it waits for the signal to bounce back. The time it takes for the signal to return tells you how far the object is. The shape of that signal tells you what the object is made of. If the object is moving, radar can tell you how fast, too. (Ask the police!)

Radar signals sent to Mars usually come back after bouncing off rocks and ice. But strangely, when radar is aimed at the Stealth Region, the signals just vanish. Maybe this area has no rocks or ice, but a lot of dust instead? Explore this region to help solve the mystery!

HERE →

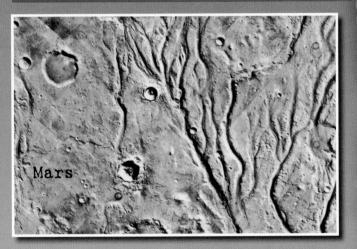

Mars

7. VALLEY NETWORKS
Claim to Fame: Oldest Rivers
Map Coordinates: M, 4

These finger-shaped valleys were carved by water about four billion years ago. That makes them the most ancient river valleys in the solar system! Valleys like these can be found in many parts of Mars. Some of the biggest ones are shown here. They are over 100 mi (160 km) long!

FIELD NOTES

How Did These Valleys Form?

Many scientists think that the valley networks on Mars were formed like most river valleys on Earth: by water flowing under open air. Since it is too cold for rivers to flow on Mars today, scientists think that its climate must have been warmer in the past.

But there's another idea. We've found valleys on Devon Island that look amazingly like the ones on Mars. These valleys were also carved by water. Except that it was not running under open air. Instead, the water flowed underneath ice covers. Maybe Mars used to have lots of ice covers, too. And maybe its climate was actually always cold.

Warm or cold, one thing is certain: The valley networks on Mars were formed by liquid water. And where there was water, there might have been life.

Devon Island

WEIRDEST ATTRACTIONS!

Over the years, spacecraft have sent back many thousands of pictures of Mars. Among them are some strange sightings. If you come across one of these weird "signs of life," just remember: They are not what they appear to be. So . . . what on Mars are they?

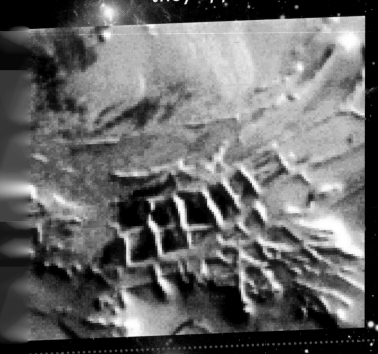

LOST CITY
COORDINATES: L, 8

Behold the remains of a city built by an ancient Martian civilization . . . NOT! We are just looking at sand piling up against volcanic rocks. The rocks are laid out in a natural grid pattern. Here's what might have happened: There was once an impact crater here with a grid of cracks underneath it. One day, hot **magma** came up from underground. It squeezed into the cracks, and then cooled and solidified. Over time, the rocks making up the crater got worn away. But the stronger volcanic rocks stayed behind. Result: bogus ruins!

ALIEN BUSHES
COORDINATES: C, 8

Do these look like bushes or what? Mars is extremely cold, too cold for any known Earth plant to grow. But could these be Martian plants adapted to survive under their planet's harsh conditions? Arthur C. Clarke, a famous science-fiction author, thought so. He caused quite a stir when he first suggested this idea in 2001. Scientists aren't sure what these "bushes" are. Their best guess: dark rocks and sand topped with icy frost.

THE FACE ON MARS

COORDINATES: N, 3

'Face on Mars" staring at the sky
ument built by Martian sculptors?
e fooled! It's just a hill with weird
ws. The same hill photographed
different lighting conditions looks
ll, just a hill!

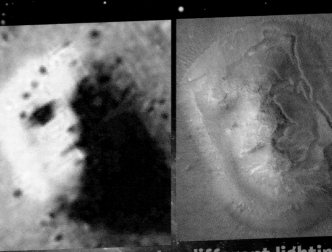

Same feature under different lighting!

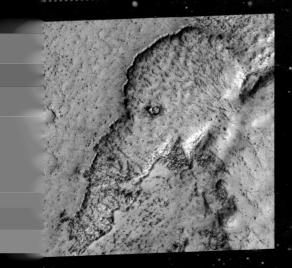

JUMBO ELEPHANT

COORDINATES: G, 3

Check out this "elephant" on Mars! This image
actually shows **lava** flows. The lava was very fluid
when it oozed out of a nearby volcano. It spread
quickly and covered large areas—almost like
floodwater. When it cooled, the lava solidified into
the shape of an elephant. By pure coincidence, of
course!

BIGFOOT ON MARS

COORDINATES: G, 5

this picture show Bigfoot on
On Earth, there are many legends
this tall, hairy, and angry apelike
e. It roams the woods or lives in the
ains. On Mars, "Bigfoot" is just a
's actually far from big. It's no more
in. (7 cm) tall!

Mars Bigfoot snapped
by the *Spirit* rover.

Earth's purported Bigfoot
caught on camera.

DIG INTO MARS

After exploring the surface of Mars, prepare to dig deeper. As you know by now, scientists think there might be plenty of water hiding deeper down in Mars. If liquid water is down there, then we might be able to find microbes living underground today. Before you pick up your shovels or drills, you need to know what the inside of Mars looks like. Basically, it's like a giant onion made up of three layers.

THE CRUST

This is the outer shell of Mars. You've been exploring just its top. For the best chance of maybe finding microbes alive today, you'll need to drill to at least 1 mi (1.6 km) below ground. The temperature in the crust increases slowly as you go. Around this depth, it might start to get warm enough for water to be liquid.

THE MANTLE

Just beneath the crust is the mantle. As you go down this massive layer, the temperature keeps rising. The pressure increases, too. What does this combo help produce? A zone made of hot, squishy rocks. If you could see mantle rocks, they would look greenish. That's because they contain a mineral called olivine, which got its name from the color of green olives.

THE CORE

This is the deepest part of Mars. It's made mostly of iron. The temperature here reaches about 2,700ºF (1,500ºC). That's very hot, but not enough to melt the solid iron.

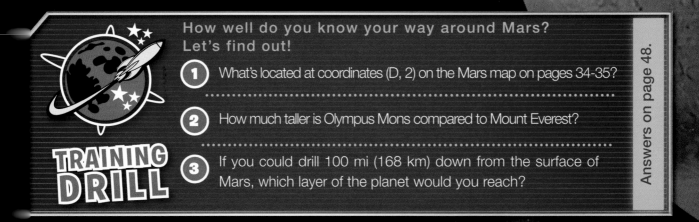

How well do you know your way around Mars? Let's find out!

1 What's located at coordinates (D, 2) on the Mars map on pages 34-35?

2 How much taller is Olympus Mons compared to Mount Everest?

3 If you could drill 100 mi (168 km) down from the surface of Mars, which layer of the planet would you reach?

Answers on page 48.

TRAINING DRILL

Diagram (left)

CRUST
30 mi (50 km)

MANTLE

1,000 mi (1,600 km)

CORE

2,100 mi (3,400 km)

Making Holes on Mars

Drilling on Mars has begun! The *Curiosity* rover is equipped with the first drill to work on Mars. But this drill is small; it's about the size of a power tool we use at home. It poked its first Mars rock on February 8, 2013.

Curiosity's Drill

Why make holes in rocks? The surface of most rocks on Mars has a rusty buildup. By poking through this layer, scientists can study what the rock is really made of.

Curiosity's drill is not long or powerful enough to drill very deep into Mars. To really dig into the planet to "Follow the Water," my colleagues at NASA Ames Research Center are working on a bigger drill. Called the Icebreaker, it's capable of drilling 10 ft (3 m) or more into ice and rock on Mars. Check out Icebreaker undergoing testing on Devon Island.

NASA Icebreaker

PLAN A NEW WORLD

COULD THIS BE NEXT?

More than one human mission will be needed for us to better understand Mars. After your visit, perhaps humans will set up a permanent research base on the planet. Generations later, as the population grows, humans might try to make Mars more livable. One wild idea is to **terraform** Mars. This means to transform the whole planet into another Terra, another Earth.

One way to terraform Mars is to artificially heat up its polar ice caps. This would release water and carbon dioxide. The atmosphere will become progressively thicker and warmer. Over time, oxygen would build up, making Mars friendlier to Earth life. Mars could transform this way. . . .

YEARS INTO THE FUTURE: 100 YEARS   500 YEARS

RED MARS

For a long time, Mars will remain deadly like it is today. Humans would first set up a permanent outpost on Mars to explore the planet in detail. No Earth plants could grow outdoors yet. Plants could grow inside a greenhouse. Indoor farming on Mars would help reduce the amount of food delivered from Earth. Humans would need a spacesuit to go outside.

GREEN MARS

Mars's atmosphere continues to thicken and warm up. Ice in the ground starts to melt. Icy ponds begin to form. Hardy plants (like algae, lichen, and moss) that don't need a lot of oxygen or water can now grow outside. The original outpost has turned into a big settlement. Humans still need to wear a spacesuit outdoors. But it's leaner and lighter because the air pressure is now higher.

MESSAGE FROM YOUR TRAINING DIRECTOR

At some point, your stay on Mars will come to an end. You'll pack up and head home. Your voyage back to Earth will be like your outbound trip, but played in reverse. Then what? Will you have discovered life on Mars? Beyond your voyage, what will we do with Mars? These are big questions that we will have to answer. In this phase, you're going to consider how human exploration might impact Mars.

FUTURE MARS EXPLORER: LET'S THINK WAY AHEAD.

1,000 YEARS

BLUE MARS

Mars's atmosphere is now much thicker and warmer. Water released from the ground forms open lakes and small seas. Trees can grow outside. The settlement has turned into a city. Humans can live outdoors in shirtsleeves, but they still need an oxygen mask to survive. That's because it will take plants many more millennia to build up enough oxygen in the atmosphere for humans to breathe normally. Mars will have become another Earth . . . almost.

Think About It

Is this the right thing to do to Mars? Some say that Mars should be left largely undisturbed, especially if it has life of its own. Others say that humans should colonize any world that they can. There are even those who think that, rather than transforming Mars, we should reengineer humans to make them adapted to live on Mars! What do you think? What should humans do to Mars?

TRAINING DRILL

You're almost done with your basic training mission. How ready are you to become a Future Mars Explorer? Let's see with this final drill. This quiz covers the entire training manual! When you're done, turn to page 48 to see if you've aced the test. Good luck!

1 Mars is the _____ planet from the Sun.

   a. third
   b. fourth
   c. sixth
   d. eighth

2 If a person weighs 150 lbs (68 kg) on Earth, about how heavy would he or she feel on Mars?

   a. 9 lbs (4 kg)
   b. 57 lbs (26 kg)
   c. 150 lbs (68 kg)
   d. 300 lbs (136 kg)

3 The atmosphere of Mars consists mostly of _____ .

   a. oxygen
   b. carbon dioxide
   c. helium
   d. nitrous oxide

4 Which of the following places on Earth makes a bad Mars analog?

   a. The Arctic
   b. Antarctica
   c. Mojave Desert
   d. Amazon Rainforest

5 _____ and _____ are the two moons of Mars.

   a. Mercury, Venus
   b. Asaph, Hall
   c. Phobos, Deimos
   d. Romeo, Juliet

6 What's one of the biggest challenges in designing a spacesuit for Mars?

   a. It has to be heavy to prevent astronauts from floating away.
   b. It must also work as a SCUBA device.
   c. It needs to double as a hovercraft.
   d. It must be lightweight and easy to move in.

7 _____ is the tallest mountain in the solar system.

   a. Olympus Mons
   b. Mount Everest
   c. Mons Huygens
   d. Vinson Massif

8 The _____ is the outermost layer of Mars.

   a. crust
   b. mantle
   c. core
   d. center

9 Which of the following can't you find on Mars today?

   a. atmosphere
   b. oceans
   c. ice
   d. sand

10 The word _____ means to transform Mars into something earthlike.

   a. terraform
   b. waterlog
   c. superplant
   d. extremophile

FINAL WORDS FROM YOUR
TRAINING DIRECTOR

FUTURE MARS EXPLORER: CONGRATULATIONS ON COMPLETING YOUR BASIC TRAINING MISSION!

As you've discovered, sending humans to Mars will be very exciting. But there's still a lot to do before that can happen. I hope you will keep up with your training and join us on this great journey.

As for me, I will continue my work to help plan the first human mission to Mars. I look forward to crossing paths with you again along the way.

BEFORE I SIGN OFF, I AWARD YOU THIS CERTIFICATE FOR A JOB WELL DONE!

◯ MARS INSTITUTE

On this date _____ the Mars Institute proudly awards this

CERTIFICATE OF ACHIEVEMENT

to _____

The recipient has successfully completed the following

FUTURE MARS EXPLORER: BASIC TRAINING

Pascal Lee

PASCAL LEE, PhD
CHAIRMAN, MARS INSTITUTE

GLOSSARY

AIR PRESSURE: Force exerted by air on the surface of objects.

ANALOG: Environment or site on Earth that is similar in some way to environmental conditions or sites on another planet.

ASTEROID: Small rocky or metallic body that orbits the Sun. It sometimes collides with other planetary bodies.

ATMOSPHERIC FRICTION: Force generated by the rubbing of air molecules against an object moving through the atmosphere.

CARGO: Goods transported onboard a vehicle, like a spacecraft.

COMET: Dirty lump of ice that orbits the Sun. It sometimes collides with other planetary bodies.

EXTREMOPHILE: Microbe that thrives in environments that would be considered extreme for most other forms of life.

FOSSIL: Preserved remains of ancient life.

GRAVITY: Force of attraction between two or several bodies. This force also gives objects their weight. For instance, Earth's gravity is the force that attracts people or things to its surface. It's what makes people feel heavy.

IMPACT CRATER: Bowl-shaped hole in the ground formed by an asteroid or a comet hitting a planetary body.

LAVA: Melted rock that flows out of a volcano and onto the surface of a planetary body. Before the melted rock reaches the surface, it's called magma.

LOW EARTH ORBIT: Region above Earth's atmosphere at an altitude between 100 mi (160 km) and 1,200 mi (2,000 km).

MAGMA: Melted rock that's underground.

MICROBE: Organism, or form of life, that is tiny. Generally it is so small that you can only see it using a microscope.

MICROGRAVITY: Gravity that's very weak, close to zero.

MICROMETEORITE: Dust-grain-size space particle made of rock and metal that can hit other objects.

ROVER: Exploration vehicle that moves across the surface of a planetary body. Most planetary rovers have wheels.

SPEED OF LIGHT: Speed at which light and radio waves travel. It's the fastest known speed in nature.

TERRAFORM: Transform a planetary body into another Terra, another Earth.

VAPOR: Gas phase of a substance.

ANSWERS

TRAINING DRILLS

PHASE 1 (page 9): 1. 68.4 lbs (31.16 kg); 2. It contains rust; 3. extremophiles

PHASE 2 (page 15): 1. false; 2. true; 3. false

PHASE 3 (page 23): 1. speed of light (186,000 mi per second, or about 300,000 km per second); 2. radiation shelter; 3. the two moons of Mars

PHASE 4 (page 32): 1. 80 mi (130 km); 2. upper deck; 3. fuel cells

PHASE 5 (page 42): 1. Utopia Planitia; 2. about 8.5 mi (14.2 km); 3. mantle

PHASE 6 (page 46): 1.b; 2.b; 3.b; 4.d; 5.c; 6.d; 7.a; 8.a; 9.b; 10.a